50 Kid-Friendly Vegetarian Dish Recipes for Home

By: Kelly Johnson

Table of Contents

- Veggie Mac and Cheese
- Mini Veggie Pizzas
- Sweet Potato Fries
- Cheesy Broccoli Tots
- Veggie Quesadillas
- Spinach and Cheese Stuffed Shells
- Veggie-Packed Marinara Sauce with Pasta
- Cauliflower Nuggets
- Zucchini Muffins
- Carrot and Hummus Wraps
- Veggie Sushi Rolls
- Rainbow Veggie Skewers
- Spinach and Cheese Enchiladas
- Chickpea Patties
- Veggie Stir-Fry with Tofu
- Roasted Veggie Tacos
- Corn and Cheese Fritters
- Veggie Lasagna
- Eggplant Parmesan
- Cheese and Veggie Stuffed Bell Peppers
- Veggie Burgers
- Stuffed Zucchini Boats
- Cheesy Spinach and Artichoke Dip with Veggie Sticks
- Veggie Loaded Baked Potatoes
- Broccoli and Cheese Casserole
- Butternut Squash Mac and Cheese
- Veggie Pasta Salad
- Sweet Corn and Zucchini Pancakes
- Cheesy Polenta Fries
- Veggie Stuffed Mushrooms
- Quinoa and Veggie Bowls
- Veggie Meatballs with Marinara Sauce
- Spinach and Cheese Pinwheels
- Baked Falafel with Cucumber Yogurt Dip
- Veggie-Packed Minestrone Soup

- Veggie Empanadas
- Spinach and Ricotta Stuffed Manicotti
- Black Bean and Corn Tacos
- Ratatouille
- Vegetable Fried Rice
- Lentil Sloppy Joes
- Veggie Stuffed Pita Pockets
- Grilled Veggie Sandwiches
- Veggie-Packed Chili
- Sweet Potato and Black Bean Enchiladas
- Baked Veggie Spring Rolls
- Avocado and Veggie Sushi Bowls
- Spinach and Feta Stuffed Pastries
- Veggie Frittata Muffins
- Roasted Vegetable and Hummus Wraps

Veggie Mac and Cheese

Ingredients:

- 2 cups elbow macaroni (or any small pasta)
- 2 cups broccoli florets, chopped
- 1 cup carrots, sliced thin
- 1 cup peas (fresh or frozen)
- 2 tablespoons butter
- 2 tablespoons all-purpose flour
- 2 cups milk
- 2 cups shredded cheddar cheese
- 1/2 teaspoon garlic powder
- 1/2 teaspoon onion powder
- Salt and pepper to taste

Instructions:

1. Cook the pasta according to package instructions. In the last 3 minutes of cooking, add the broccoli and carrots to the boiling pasta water. Drain and set aside.
2. In a medium saucepan, melt the butter over medium heat. Stir in the flour and cook for 1-2 minutes until it forms a smooth paste.
3. Gradually add the milk, stirring constantly to avoid lumps. Cook until the mixture thickens, about 5 minutes.
4. Stir in the shredded cheddar cheese until melted and smooth.
5. Add the garlic powder, onion powder, salt, and pepper. Mix well.
6. Combine the cooked pasta and vegetables with the cheese sauce. Stir in the peas.
7. Serve warm and enjoy!

This recipe blends classic mac and cheese with nutritious veggies, making it a favorite for kids and adults alike.

Mini Veggie Pizzas

Ingredients:

- 4 whole wheat English muffins, split in half (or mini pita breads)
- 1 cup pizza sauce
- 1 cup shredded mozzarella cheese
- 1/2 cup cherry tomatoes, halved
- 1/2 cup bell peppers, diced (red, yellow, or green)
- 1/2 cup baby spinach, chopped
- 1/4 cup black olives, sliced
- 1/4 cup red onion, finely chopped
- 1 teaspoon dried oregano
- 1 teaspoon dried basil
- Olive oil for drizzling

Instructions:

1. Preheat the oven to 375°F (190°C).
2. Place the English muffin halves (or mini pita breads) on a baking sheet.
3. Spread a tablespoon of pizza sauce on each muffin half.
4. Sprinkle shredded mozzarella cheese evenly over the sauce.
5. Top with cherry tomatoes, bell peppers, baby spinach, black olives, and red onion.
6. Sprinkle with dried oregano and basil.
7. Drizzle a little olive oil over each mini pizza.
8. Bake in the preheated oven for 10-12 minutes, or until the cheese is melted and bubbly.
9. Let cool slightly before serving.

These Mini Veggie Pizzas are perfect for little hands and are fun to make and eat!

Sweet Potato Fries

Ingredients:

- 2 large sweet potatoes
- 2 tablespoons olive oil
- 1 teaspoon paprika
- 1 teaspoon garlic powder
- 1/2 teaspoon salt
- 1/2 teaspoon black pepper
- 1/2 teaspoon cinnamon (optional for a sweet twist)

Instructions:

1. Preheat your oven to 425°F (220°C).
2. Peel the sweet potatoes and cut them into thin, even-sized strips.
3. Place the sweet potato strips in a large bowl. Drizzle with olive oil and toss to coat evenly.
4. In a small bowl, mix together the paprika, garlic powder, salt, black pepper, and cinnamon (if using).
5. Sprinkle the seasoning mixture over the sweet potatoes and toss to ensure all fries are well coated.
6. Spread the sweet potato fries out in a single layer on a baking sheet lined with parchment paper.
7. Bake for 25-30 minutes, flipping halfway through, until the fries are golden and crispy.
8. Remove from the oven and let them cool slightly before serving.

These Sweet Potato Fries are a delicious and healthy alternative to regular fries, perfect for kids and adults alike!

Cheesy Broccoli Tots

Ingredients:

- 2 cups broccoli florets (fresh or frozen)
- 1 cup shredded cheddar cheese
- 1/2 cup breadcrumbs (whole wheat or regular)
- 1/4 cup grated Parmesan cheese
- 1 large egg
- 1/2 teaspoon garlic powder
- 1/2 teaspoon onion powder
- Salt and pepper to taste
- Olive oil for drizzling

Instructions:

1. Preheat your oven to 400°F (200°C). Line a baking sheet with parchment paper.
2. If using fresh broccoli, steam the florets until tender (about 5 minutes). If using frozen broccoli, cook according to package instructions. Drain and let cool.
3. Finely chop the broccoli or pulse it in a food processor until it resembles rice.
4. In a large bowl, combine the chopped broccoli, shredded cheddar cheese, breadcrumbs, grated Parmesan cheese, egg, garlic powder, onion powder, salt, and pepper. Mix well until all ingredients are evenly incorporated.
5. Scoop about 1 tablespoon of the mixture and form it into a small tot shape. Place the tots on the prepared baking sheet. Repeat with the remaining mixture.
6. Lightly drizzle the tots with olive oil.
7. Bake in the preheated oven for 20-25 minutes, turning them halfway through, until the tots are golden brown and crispy.
8. Let the tots cool slightly before serving.

These Cheesy Broccoli Tots are a fun and tasty way to get kids to eat their veggies!

Veggie Quesadillas

Ingredients:

- 4 large whole wheat tortillas
- 1 cup shredded cheddar cheese
- 1 cup shredded Monterey Jack cheese
- 1 cup bell peppers, diced (red, yellow, or green)
- 1 cup zucchini, diced
- 1/2 cup corn kernels (fresh or frozen)
- 1/2 cup black beans, drained and rinsed
- 1/4 cup red onion, finely chopped
- 1 tablespoon olive oil
- 1 teaspoon ground cumin
- 1/2 teaspoon chili powder
- Salt and pepper to taste
- Sour cream, salsa, and guacamole for serving (optional)

Instructions:

1. In a large skillet, heat the olive oil over medium heat.
2. Add the bell peppers, zucchini, corn, and red onion. Sauté for about 5 minutes until the vegetables are tender.
3. Add the black beans, ground cumin, chili powder, salt, and pepper. Stir to combine and cook for an additional 2-3 minutes. Remove from heat.
4. Heat a clean, large skillet or griddle over medium heat.
5. Place one tortilla in the skillet and sprinkle half of the shredded cheddar and Monterey Jack cheese evenly over the tortilla.
6. Spoon half of the veggie mixture over the cheese layer.
7. Sprinkle the remaining cheese on top of the veggies, then cover with another tortilla.
8. Cook for 2-3 minutes on each side, or until the tortilla is golden brown and the cheese is melted.
9. Remove the quesadilla from the skillet and let it cool slightly before cutting into wedges.
10. Repeat the process with the remaining ingredients to make the second quesadilla.
11. Serve the veggie quesadillas warm with sour cream, salsa, and guacamole on the side, if desired.

These Veggie Quesadillas are easy to make and packed with delicious vegetables, making them a hit with kids and adults alike!

Spinach and Cheese Stuffed Shells

Ingredients:

- 20 jumbo pasta shells
- 2 cups ricotta cheese
- 1 cup shredded mozzarella cheese, divided
- 1/2 cup grated Parmesan cheese
- 1 egg, beaten
- 2 cups fresh spinach, chopped (or 1 cup frozen spinach, thawed and drained)
- 2 cups marinara sauce
- 1 teaspoon garlic powder
- 1 teaspoon dried basil
- 1/2 teaspoon salt
- 1/2 teaspoon black pepper

Instructions:

1. Preheat your oven to 375°F (190°C).
2. Cook the jumbo pasta shells according to the package instructions until al dente. Drain and rinse with cold water to prevent sticking. Set aside.
3. In a large bowl, combine the ricotta cheese, 1/2 cup shredded mozzarella cheese, grated Parmesan cheese, beaten egg, chopped spinach, garlic powder, dried basil, salt, and pepper. Mix well.
4. Spread 1 cup of marinara sauce evenly in the bottom of a 9x13-inch baking dish.
5. Stuff each cooked pasta shell with the spinach and cheese mixture and place them in the baking dish, open side up.
6. Pour the remaining 1 cup of marinara sauce over the stuffed shells.
7. Sprinkle the remaining 1/2 cup of shredded mozzarella cheese on top.
8. Cover the baking dish with aluminum foil and bake for 25 minutes.
9. Remove the foil and bake for an additional 10 minutes, or until the cheese is bubbly and slightly golden.
10. Let the stuffed shells cool for a few minutes before serving.

These Spinach and Cheese Stuffed Shells are a delicious and nutritious meal that kids will love!

Veggie-Packed Marinara Sauce with Pasta

Ingredients:

- 1 pound pasta (spaghetti, penne, or your favorite type)
- 2 tablespoons olive oil
- 1 onion, finely chopped
- 2 garlic cloves, minced
- 1 carrot, finely chopped
- 1 zucchini, finely chopped
- 1 red bell pepper, finely chopped
- 1 cup mushrooms, chopped
- 1 can (28 ounces) crushed tomatoes
- 1 can (14.5 ounces) diced tomatoes
- 1 teaspoon dried basil
- 1 teaspoon dried oregano
- 1/2 teaspoon salt
- 1/2 teaspoon black pepper
- 1 teaspoon sugar (optional, to balance acidity)
- 1/4 cup fresh basil, chopped (optional, for garnish)
- Grated Parmesan cheese (optional, for serving)

Instructions:

1. Cook the pasta according to the package instructions. Drain and set aside.
2. In a large skillet or saucepan, heat the olive oil over medium heat.
3. Add the onion and garlic, and sauté until the onion is translucent, about 5 minutes.
4. Add the carrot, zucchini, red bell pepper, and mushrooms. Cook until the vegetables are tender, about 7-10 minutes.
5. Stir in the crushed tomatoes and diced tomatoes (with their juice).
6. Add the dried basil, dried oregano, salt, black pepper, and sugar (if using). Stir to combine.
7. Bring the sauce to a simmer and let it cook for about 20 minutes, stirring occasionally, until the flavors are well combined and the sauce has thickened.
8. Taste and adjust seasoning if necessary.
9. Serve the veggie-packed marinara sauce over the cooked pasta.
10. Garnish with fresh basil and grated Parmesan cheese, if desired.

This Veggie-Packed Marinara Sauce with Pasta is a nutritious and delicious meal that is sure to be a hit with kids and adults alike!

Cauliflower Nuggets

Ingredients:

- 1 large head of cauliflower, cut into bite-sized florets
- 1 cup all-purpose flour (or a gluten-free flour blend)
- 1 teaspoon garlic powder
- 1 teaspoon onion powder
- 1 teaspoon paprika
- 1/2 teaspoon salt
- 1/2 teaspoon black pepper
- 1 cup milk (dairy or plant-based)
- 2 cups breadcrumbs (panko or regular)
- Olive oil spray or a small amount of oil for baking

Instructions:

1. Preheat your oven to 400°F (200°C). Line a baking sheet with parchment paper or lightly grease it.
2. In a large bowl, whisk together the flour, garlic powder, onion powder, paprika, salt, and black pepper.
3. Add the milk to the flour mixture and whisk until smooth to create the batter.
4. Place the breadcrumbs in a separate bowl.
5. Dip each cauliflower floret into the batter, allowing any excess to drip off, then roll it in the breadcrumbs until well-coated. Place the coated florets on the prepared baking sheet.
6. Lightly spray or drizzle the cauliflower nuggets with olive oil.
7. Bake for 25-30 minutes, flipping halfway through, until the nuggets are golden brown and crispy.
8. Let cool slightly before serving.

These Cauliflower Nuggets are a healthy and tasty alternative to traditional nuggets, making them perfect for kids and adults alike! Serve with your favorite dipping sauces such as ketchup, ranch, or BBQ sauce.

Zucchini Muffins

Ingredients:

- 1 1/2 cups all-purpose flour
- 1 teaspoon baking powder
- 1/2 teaspoon baking soda
- 1/2 teaspoon salt
- 1 teaspoon ground cinnamon
- 1/2 teaspoon ground nutmeg
- 1/4 cup unsalted butter, melted and cooled
- 1/2 cup granulated sugar
- 1/4 cup brown sugar, packed
- 1/4 cup plain yogurt (Greek yogurt or regular)
- 1 teaspoon vanilla extract
- 1 large egg
- 1 1/2 cups grated zucchini (about 1 medium zucchini)
- 1/2 cup chopped walnuts or pecans (optional)

Instructions:

1. Preheat your oven to 350°F (175°C). Line a muffin tin with paper liners or grease the muffin cups.
2. In a medium bowl, whisk together the flour, baking powder, baking soda, salt, cinnamon, and nutmeg.
3. In a separate large bowl, whisk together the melted butter, granulated sugar, brown sugar, yogurt, vanilla extract, and egg until well combined.
4. Fold the grated zucchini into the wet ingredients.
5. Add the dry ingredients to the wet ingredients and gently fold together until just combined. Be careful not to overmix.
6. If using, gently fold in the chopped nuts.
7. Divide the batter evenly among the muffin cups, filling each about 3/4 full.
8. Bake for 18-22 minutes, or until a toothpick inserted into the center comes out clean.
9. Allow the muffins to cool in the pan for 5 minutes before transferring them to a wire rack to cool completely.

Enjoy these Zucchini Muffins warm or at room temperature. They're perfect for breakfast, snacks, or even packed lunches for kids!

Carrot and Hummus Wraps

Ingredients:

- 4 large whole wheat or spinach wraps (or tortillas)
- 1 cup hummus (store-bought or homemade)
- 2 cups shredded carrots
- 1/2 cup baby spinach leaves
- 1/4 cup sliced cucumber
- 1/4 cup sliced red bell pepper
- 1/4 cup crumbled feta cheese (optional)
- Salt and pepper to taste

Instructions:

1. Lay out the wraps on a clean surface.
2. Spread about 1/4 cup of hummus evenly onto each wrap, leaving a small border around the edges.
3. Divide the shredded carrots, baby spinach leaves, sliced cucumber, and sliced red bell pepper evenly among the wraps, arranging them in a line down the center of each wrap.
4. If using, sprinkle the crumbled feta cheese evenly over the vegetables.
5. Season with salt and pepper to taste.
6. Fold in the sides of each wrap, then roll them up tightly from the bottom to enclose the filling.
7. Slice each wrap in half diagonally, if desired, and serve immediately.

These Carrot and Hummus Wraps are packed with crunchy vegetables and creamy hummus, making them a tasty and healthy option for lunch or a quick snack on the go. Adjust the fillings according to your preferences or add a drizzle of your favorite dressing for extra flavor!

Veggie Sushi Rolls

Ingredients:

- 4 sheets of nori (seaweed sheets)
- 2 cups sushi rice, cooked and seasoned with rice vinegar, sugar, and salt
- 1/2 cucumber, cut into thin strips
- 1/2 avocado, thinly sliced
- 1/2 carrot, cut into thin matchsticks
- 1/2 bell pepper (red, yellow, or green), thinly sliced
- 1/4 cup shredded or thinly sliced cabbage
- Soy sauce, pickled ginger, and wasabi for serving (optional)

Instructions:

1. Place a sheet of nori shiny side down on a bamboo sushi mat or a clean kitchen towel.
2. With wet hands, spread about 1/2 cup of sushi rice evenly over the nori sheet, leaving a 1-inch border at the top.
3. Arrange a layer of cucumber strips, avocado slices, carrot matchsticks, bell pepper slices, and shredded cabbage in a line across the center of the rice.
4. Using the bamboo mat or towel, carefully roll the nori sheet over the filling, starting from the bottom edge closest to you. Use gentle pressure to shape the roll.
5. Seal the edge of the nori sheet with a little water to help it stick together.
6. Repeat with the remaining nori sheets and filling ingredients.
7. Using a sharp knife, slice each sushi roll into 6-8 pieces.
8. Arrange the Veggie Sushi Rolls on a serving plate and serve with soy sauce, pickled ginger, and wasabi on the side, if desired.

These Veggie Sushi Rolls are customizable, healthy, and perfect for a light lunch, snack, or even as part of a party platter. Enjoy the fresh flavors and crunchy textures!

Rainbow Veggie Skewers

Ingredients:

- 1 red bell pepper, cut into chunks
- 1 orange bell pepper, cut into chunks
- 1 yellow bell pepper, cut into chunks
- 1 green bell pepper, cut into chunks
- 1 small red onion, cut into chunks
- 1 zucchini, sliced into rounds
- 1 yellow squash, sliced into rounds
- 8-10 cherry tomatoes
- Wooden skewers, soaked in water for 30 minutes (to prevent burning)

Instructions:

1. Preheat your grill or grill pan over medium-high heat.
2. Assemble the skewers by threading the vegetables onto the skewers in a rainbow pattern, alternating colors. Leave a little space between each piece to ensure even cooking.
3. Brush the assembled skewers with olive oil and season with salt and pepper, or your favorite seasoning blend.
4. Place the skewers on the preheated grill or grill pan. Cook for about 3-4 minutes on each side, or until the vegetables are tender and lightly charred.
5. Remove the skewers from the grill and serve immediately.

These Rainbow Veggie Skewers are not only visually appealing but also packed with flavor and nutrients. They make a fantastic side dish for grilled meats, fish, or tofu, or they can be enjoyed on their own as a light and colorful vegetarian meal.

Spinach and Cheese Enchiladas

Ingredients:

- 10-12 corn or flour tortillas
- 1 tablespoon olive oil
- 1 small onion, finely chopped
- 3 cloves garlic, minced
- 8 cups fresh spinach leaves
- 1 can (15 ounces) black beans, drained and rinsed
- 1 cup corn kernels (fresh, frozen, or canned)
- 2 cups shredded Monterey Jack cheese or Mexican blend cheese, divided
- 1 can (15 ounces) enchilada sauce (red or green)
- Salt and pepper, to taste
- Fresh cilantro, chopped, for garnish (optional)
- Sour cream, salsa, and guacamole, for serving (optional)

Instructions:

1. Preheat your oven to 375°F (190°C). Grease a 9x13-inch baking dish.
2. In a large skillet, heat the olive oil over medium heat. Add the chopped onion and cook until softened, about 5 minutes.
3. Add the minced garlic and cook for an additional 1-2 minutes until fragrant.
4. Stir in the fresh spinach leaves and cook until wilted, about 2-3 minutes. Season with salt and pepper.
5. Remove the skillet from heat and stir in the black beans, corn kernels, and 1 cup of shredded cheese until well combined.
6. Warm the tortillas briefly in a microwave or on a dry skillet to make them pliable.
7. Spoon a generous amount of the spinach and cheese filling into each tortilla, roll them up, and place them seam-side down in the prepared baking dish.
8. Pour the enchilada sauce evenly over the rolled tortillas.
9. Sprinkle the remaining 1 cup of shredded cheese over the top of the enchiladas.
10. Cover the baking dish with aluminum foil and bake for 20 minutes.
11. Remove the foil and bake for an additional 10 minutes, or until the cheese is melted and bubbly.
12. Remove from the oven and let the enchiladas cool slightly before serving.
13. Garnish with chopped fresh cilantro, if desired, and serve with sour cream, salsa, and guacamole on the side.

These Spinach and Cheese Enchiladas are comforting, packed with nutritious ingredients, and perfect for a family dinner or gathering with friends. Enjoy the flavors and textures with your favorite Mexican-inspired toppings!

Chickpea Patties

Ingredients:

- 2 cans (15 ounces each) chickpeas, drained and rinsed
- 1 small onion, finely chopped
- 2 cloves garlic, minced
- 1/2 cup breadcrumbs (panko or regular)
- 1/4 cup chopped fresh parsley
- 1 teaspoon ground cumin
- 1 teaspoon ground coriander
- 1/2 teaspoon paprika
- 1/2 teaspoon salt
- 1/4 teaspoon black pepper
- 1/4 cup all-purpose flour (or chickpea flour for gluten-free option)
- Olive oil, for frying

Instructions:

1. In a food processor, pulse the chickpeas until they are coarsely chopped. You want some texture remaining, not a smooth paste.
2. Transfer the chopped chickpeas to a large mixing bowl.
3. Add the chopped onion, minced garlic, breadcrumbs, parsley, ground cumin, ground coriander, paprika, salt, and black pepper to the bowl with the chickpeas. Mix well to combine all ingredients evenly.
4. Shape the mixture into patties using about 1/4 cup of the mixture for each patty. If the mixture seems too wet, add a little more breadcrumbs or flour to bind it together.
5. Heat a thin layer of olive oil in a large skillet over medium heat.
6. Dredge each patty lightly in flour, shaking off any excess.
7. Place the patties in the skillet and cook for about 4-5 minutes on each side, or until golden brown and crispy.
8. Remove the patties from the skillet and place them on a plate lined with paper towels to absorb excess oil.
9. Serve the chickpea patties warm with your favorite toppings or sauces, such as tzatziki, hummus, or a yogurt-based sauce with herbs.

These Chickpea Patties are delicious as a main dish served with a salad or as a sandwich filling. They're packed with protein and flavor, making them a great vegetarian option for lunch or dinner!

Veggie Stir-Fry with Tofu

Ingredients:

- 14 oz (400g) firm tofu, drained and cut into cubes
- 2 tablespoons soy sauce
- 1 tablespoon cornstarch
- 2 tablespoons vegetable oil, divided
- 1 onion, sliced
- 2 bell peppers (any color), sliced
- 1 cup broccoli florets
- 1 cup snow peas or sugar snap peas
- 1 cup sliced mushrooms (shiitake, button, or cremini)
- 3 cloves garlic, minced
- 1-inch piece of ginger, grated
- 1/4 cup vegetable broth or water
- 2 tablespoons hoisin sauce
- 1 tablespoon rice vinegar
- 1 tablespoon sesame oil
- Cooked rice or noodles, for serving
- Sesame seeds and chopped green onions, for garnish (optional)

Instructions:

1. In a bowl, toss the tofu cubes with soy sauce and cornstarch until evenly coated.
2. Heat 1 tablespoon of vegetable oil in a large skillet or wok over medium-high heat. Add the tofu cubes and cook until golden and crispy on all sides, about 5-7 minutes. Remove tofu from skillet and set aside.
3. In the same skillet, add the remaining tablespoon of vegetable oil. Add the sliced onion and bell peppers. Stir-fry for 2-3 minutes until slightly softened.
4. Add the broccoli florets, snow peas, and mushrooms to the skillet. Cook for another 3-4 minutes until the vegetables are tender-crisp.
5. Add the minced garlic and grated ginger to the skillet. Stir-fry for 1 minute until fragrant.
6. Return the cooked tofu to the skillet.
7. In a small bowl, whisk together the vegetable broth (or water), hoisin sauce, rice vinegar, and sesame oil. Pour this sauce over the tofu and vegetables in the skillet.
8. Stir everything together gently to coat evenly. Cook for another 1-2 minutes until heated through.
9. Serve the veggie stir-fry with tofu over cooked rice or noodles.
10. Garnish with sesame seeds and chopped green onions, if desired.

This Veggie Stir-Fry with Tofu is colorful, flavorful, and packed with protein and vegetables. It's a perfect dish for a quick and healthy vegetarian meal!

Roasted Veggie Tacos

Ingredients:

- 1 large bell pepper, sliced
- 1 medium zucchini, sliced
- 1 medium yellow squash, sliced
- 1 small red onion, sliced
- 1 cup cherry tomatoes, halved
- 2 tablespoons olive oil
- 1 teaspoon ground cumin
- 1 teaspoon chili powder
- 1/2 teaspoon smoked paprika
- Salt and pepper, to taste
- 8-10 small corn or flour tortillas
- Toppings: diced avocado, chopped cilantro, crumbled feta or cotija cheese, lime wedges, salsa, sour cream (optional)

Instructions:

1. Preheat your oven to 400°F (200°C). Line a baking sheet with parchment paper.
2. In a large bowl, combine the sliced bell pepper, zucchini, yellow squash, red onion, and cherry tomatoes.
3. Drizzle olive oil over the vegetables and sprinkle with ground cumin, chili powder, smoked paprika, salt, and pepper. Toss to coat evenly.
4. Spread the seasoned vegetables in a single layer on the prepared baking sheet.
5. Roast in the preheated oven for 20-25 minutes, stirring halfway through, until the vegetables are tender and slightly charred.
6. While the vegetables are roasting, warm the tortillas in a dry skillet or wrap them in foil and heat them in the oven for a few minutes.
7. Assemble the tacos by spooning roasted vegetables onto each tortilla.
8. Add your desired toppings such as diced avocado, chopped cilantro, crumbled feta or cotija cheese, and a squeeze of lime juice.
9. Serve the roasted veggie tacos immediately with salsa and sour cream on the side, if desired.

These Roasted Veggie Tacos are colorful, flavorful, and versatile. They make a satisfying vegetarian meal that's perfect for weeknight dinners or gatherings with friends and family. Enjoy the delicious combination of roasted vegetables and your favorite taco toppings!

Corn and Cheese Fritters

Ingredients:

- 1 cup corn kernels (fresh, frozen, or canned)
- 1/2 cup shredded cheddar cheese
- 1/4 cup grated Parmesan cheese
- 1/4 cup all-purpose flour
- 1/4 cup cornmeal (or breadcrumbs)
- 1/4 cup chopped fresh parsley or cilantro
- 2 green onions, finely chopped
- 1/2 teaspoon baking powder
- 1/2 teaspoon paprika
- 1/4 teaspoon salt
- 1/4 teaspoon black pepper
- 1 large egg, lightly beaten
- 2-3 tablespoons milk or buttermilk
- Vegetable oil, for frying

Instructions:

1. In a large bowl, combine the corn kernels, shredded cheddar cheese, grated Parmesan cheese, flour, cornmeal (or breadcrumbs), chopped parsley or cilantro, green onions, baking powder, paprika, salt, and black pepper.
2. Stir in the lightly beaten egg and 2 tablespoons of milk or buttermilk. Mix until all ingredients are well combined. If the mixture seems too dry, add the remaining tablespoon of milk or buttermilk as needed to achieve a thick batter consistency.
3. Heat vegetable oil in a large skillet over medium heat.
4. Drop spoonfuls of the corn and cheese batter into the skillet, using about 2 tablespoons of batter for each fritter. Flatten slightly with the back of a spoon.
5. Fry the fritters in batches for about 2-3 minutes on each side, or until golden brown and crispy.
6. Remove the fritters from the skillet and place them on a plate lined with paper towels to absorb excess oil.
7. Serve the corn and cheese fritters warm, optionally with a dipping sauce like sour cream mixed with salsa or a spicy aioli.

These Corn and Cheese Fritters make a delicious appetizer, snack, or side dish. They're packed with sweet corn kernels and cheesy goodness, perfect for any occasion!

Veggie Lasagna

Ingredients:

- 9 lasagna noodles (oven-ready or cooked according to package instructions)
- 1 tablespoon olive oil
- 1 onion, diced
- 3 cloves garlic, minced
- 1 medium zucchini, diced
- 1 medium yellow squash, diced
- 1 red bell pepper, diced
- 1 cup sliced mushrooms (any variety)
- 1 (24-ounce) jar marinara sauce
- 1 (15-ounce) container ricotta cheese
- 1 cup shredded mozzarella cheese
- 1/2 cup grated Parmesan cheese
- 1/4 cup chopped fresh basil or parsley
- Salt and pepper, to taste

Instructions:

1. Preheat your oven to 375°F (190°C). Grease a 9x13-inch baking dish.
2. Heat olive oil in a large skillet over medium heat. Add diced onion and cook until translucent, about 5 minutes.
3. Add minced garlic and cook for another 1-2 minutes until fragrant.
4. Add diced zucchini, yellow squash, red bell pepper, and sliced mushrooms to the skillet. Cook for 5-7 minutes until vegetables are tender. Season with salt and pepper to taste.
5. Stir in the marinara sauce and simmer for 5 minutes. Remove from heat and set aside.
6. In a medium bowl, combine ricotta cheese, shredded mozzarella cheese, grated Parmesan cheese, chopped basil or parsley, salt, and pepper. Mix until well combined.
7. To assemble the lasagna, spread a thin layer of the vegetable marinara sauce on the bottom of the prepared baking dish.
8. Place 3 lasagna noodles over the sauce. Spread half of the ricotta cheese mixture evenly over the noodles.
9. Spoon half of the remaining vegetable marinara sauce over the ricotta layer.
10. Repeat with another layer of 3 lasagna noodles, the remaining ricotta cheese mixture, and the remaining vegetable marinara sauce.
11. Top with the final layer of 3 lasagna noodles and spread any remaining sauce over the top. Sprinkle with additional shredded mozzarella cheese and grated Parmesan cheese, if desired.
12. Cover the baking dish with aluminum foil and bake in the preheated oven for 30 minutes.
13. Remove the foil and bake for an additional 10-15 minutes, or until the cheese is bubbly and golden brown.
14. Let the veggie lasagna cool for 10-15 minutes before slicing and serving.

This Veggie Lasagna is a wholesome and satisfying dish that's perfect for feeding a crowd or enjoying leftovers throughout the week. It's packed with nutritious vegetables and layers of cheesy goodness!

Eggplant Parmesan

Ingredients:

- 2 medium eggplants, sliced into 1/2-inch rounds
- Salt
- 1 cup all-purpose flour
- 3 large eggs, beaten
- 2 cups breadcrumbs (panko or regular)
- 1/2 cup grated Parmesan cheese, plus extra for serving
- 2 cups marinara sauce
- 1 cup shredded mozzarella cheese
- Fresh basil leaves, chopped, for garnish (optional)
- Olive oil, for frying

Instructions:

1. Preheat your oven to 375°F (190°C). Grease a 9x13-inch baking dish.
2. Place the eggplant slices in a colander and sprinkle generously with salt. Let them sit for about 20-30 minutes to release excess moisture. Pat dry with paper towels.
3. Set up a breading station: Place the flour in one shallow dish, beaten eggs in another dish, and breadcrumbs mixed with grated Parmesan cheese in a third dish.
4. Dredge each eggplant slice in flour, shaking off any excess. Dip into the beaten eggs, allowing any excess to drip off. Finally, coat evenly with the breadcrumb mixture, pressing gently to adhere.
5. Heat a generous amount of olive oil in a large skillet over medium-high heat. Fry the breaded eggplant slices in batches until golden brown and crispy on both sides, about 2-3 minutes per side. Add more oil as needed between batches. Drain on paper towels.
6. Spread a thin layer of marinara sauce on the bottom of the prepared baking dish.
7. Arrange half of the fried eggplant slices in a single layer over the marinara sauce.
8. Spoon more marinara sauce over each eggplant slice, then sprinkle with shredded mozzarella cheese.
9. Repeat with another layer of the remaining eggplant slices, marinara sauce, and shredded mozzarella cheese.
10. Sprinkle extra grated Parmesan cheese over the top.
11. Cover the baking dish with aluminum foil and bake in the preheated oven for 25 minutes.
12. Remove the foil and bake for an additional 10 minutes, or until the cheese is melted and bubbly.
13. Let the Eggplant Parmesan cool for a few minutes before serving.
14. Garnish with chopped fresh basil leaves, if desired, and serve hot with additional marinara sauce and grated Parmesan cheese on the side.

This Eggplant Parmesan is delicious served with a side of pasta or a fresh green salad. It's a comforting and flavorful dish that's sure to become a family favorite!

Cheese and Veggie Stuffed Bell Peppers

Ingredients:

- 4 large bell peppers (any color), tops cut off and seeds removed
- 1 tablespoon olive oil
- 1 onion, diced
- 2 cloves garlic, minced
- 1 zucchini, diced
- 1 yellow squash, diced
- 1 cup corn kernels (fresh, frozen, or canned)
- 1 cup cooked quinoa or rice
- 1 cup shredded cheddar cheese or Mexican blend cheese, divided
- 1 teaspoon dried oregano
- 1 teaspoon ground cumin
- Salt and pepper, to taste
- Fresh parsley or cilantro, chopped, for garnish (optional)

Instructions:

1. Preheat your oven to 375°F (190°C). Grease a baking dish large enough to hold the bell peppers upright.
2. Heat olive oil in a large skillet over medium heat. Add diced onion and cook until translucent, about 5 minutes.
3. Add minced garlic and cook for another 1-2 minutes until fragrant.
4. Add diced zucchini, yellow squash, and corn kernels to the skillet. Cook for 5-7 minutes until vegetables are tender.
5. Stir in cooked quinoa or rice, half of the shredded cheese, dried oregano, ground cumin, salt, and pepper. Mix until well combined and cheese is melted. Remove from heat.
6. Spoon the vegetable and quinoa (or rice) mixture evenly into each hollowed-out bell pepper.
7. Sprinkle the remaining shredded cheese evenly over the stuffed bell peppers.
8. Place the stuffed bell peppers upright in the prepared baking dish.
9. Cover the dish loosely with aluminum foil and bake in the preheated oven for 30-35 minutes, or until the bell peppers are tender.
10. Remove the foil and bake for an additional 5 minutes, or until the cheese is melted and bubbly.
11. Remove from the oven and let the stuffed bell peppers cool for a few minutes before serving.
12. Garnish with chopped fresh parsley or cilantro, if desired, and serve hot.

These Cheese and Veggie Stuffed Bell Peppers are a nutritious and satisfying vegetarian meal. They're packed with flavors from the vegetables, quinoa (or rice), and melted cheese, making them a delicious option for lunch or dinner!

Veggie Burgers

Ingredients:

- 1 can (15 ounces) black beans, drained and rinsed
- 1 cup cooked quinoa or brown rice
- 1 cup cooked sweet potatoes, mashed
- 1/2 cup finely chopped bell peppers (any color)
- 1/2 cup finely chopped onion
- 2 cloves garlic, minced
- 1 teaspoon ground cumin
- 1 teaspoon paprika
- 1/2 teaspoon chili powder
- Salt and pepper, to taste
- 1/2 cup breadcrumbs (panko or regular)
- 1/4 cup chopped fresh cilantro or parsley
- 1 tablespoon soy sauce or tamari (for gluten-free option)
- 1 tablespoon olive oil, plus more for cooking
- Hamburger buns or lettuce wraps, for serving
- Toppings of choice: lettuce, tomato slices, avocado, cheese (optional)

Instructions:

1. In a large bowl, mash the black beans with a fork or potato masher until mostly smooth, leaving some texture.
2. Add cooked quinoa or brown rice, mashed sweet potatoes, chopped bell peppers, chopped onion, minced garlic, ground cumin, paprika, chili powder, salt, and pepper to the bowl with the mashed beans. Mix well to combine.
3. Stir in breadcrumbs, chopped cilantro or parsley, soy sauce (or tamari), and olive oil until the mixture is evenly combined and holds together when pressed.
4. Divide the mixture into 4-6 portions, depending on how large you want your burgers.
5. Shape each portion into a patty using your hands. If the mixture feels too wet, add more breadcrumbs; if too dry, add a little more olive oil or water.
6. Heat a tablespoon of olive oil in a large skillet over medium heat.
7. Cook the veggie burgers for about 4-5 minutes on each side, or until golden brown and heated through.
8. If using cheese, place a slice on top of each burger during the last minute of cooking and cover the skillet with a lid to melt the cheese.
9. Serve the veggie burgers on hamburger buns or lettuce wraps, topped with your favorite toppings such as lettuce, tomato slices, avocado, and any additional condiments.

These homemade Veggie Burgers are flavorful, packed with wholesome ingredients, and customizable to suit your taste preferences. They're a delicious and satisfying option for a meatless meal!

Stuffed Zucchini Boats

Ingredients:

- 4 medium zucchini
- 1 tablespoon olive oil
- 1 small onion, finely chopped
- 2 cloves garlic, minced
- 1 bell pepper (any color), diced
- 1 cup diced tomatoes (fresh or canned)
- 1 cup cooked quinoa or rice
- 1/2 cup shredded mozzarella cheese, divided
- 1/4 cup grated Parmesan cheese
- 1 teaspoon dried oregano
- Salt and pepper, to taste
- Fresh basil or parsley, chopped, for garnish (optional)

Instructions:

1. Preheat your oven to 400°F (200°C). Grease a baking dish large enough to hold the zucchini boats.
2. Cut each zucchini in half lengthwise. Use a spoon to scoop out the flesh, leaving about 1/4-inch thick shells. Reserve the flesh in a bowl.
3. Heat olive oil in a large skillet over medium heat. Add chopped onion and cook until translucent, about 5 minutes.
4. Add minced garlic and diced bell pepper to the skillet. Cook for another 2-3 minutes until bell pepper is slightly softened.
5. Chop the reserved zucchini flesh and add it to the skillet. Cook for 3-4 minutes until zucchini is tender.
6. Stir in diced tomatoes, cooked quinoa or rice, half of the shredded mozzarella cheese, grated Parmesan cheese, dried oregano, salt, and pepper. Mix until well combined and heated through. Remove from heat.
7. Spoon the filling mixture evenly into the hollowed-out zucchini halves, pressing gently to fill each boat.
8. Sprinkle the remaining shredded mozzarella cheese over the stuffed zucchini boats.
9. Place the stuffed zucchini boats in the prepared baking dish. Cover with foil and bake in the preheated oven for 20-25 minutes, or until zucchini is tender.
10. Remove the foil and bake for an additional 5 minutes, or until cheese is melted and bubbly.
11. Remove from the oven and let the stuffed zucchini boats cool for a few minutes before serving.
12. Garnish with chopped fresh basil or parsley, if desired, and serve hot.

These Stuffed Zucchini Boats make a satisfying and nutritious meal, perfect for a vegetarian dinner option. They're filled with a flavorful mixture of vegetables, grains, and cheese, making them a delicious and wholesome dish!

Cheesy Spinach and Artichoke Dip with Veggie Sticks

Ingredients:

- 1 tablespoon olive oil
- 1 small onion, finely chopped
- 2 cloves garlic, minced
- 1 (10-ounce) package frozen chopped spinach, thawed and drained
- 1 (14-ounce) can artichoke hearts, drained and chopped
- 1 (8-ounce) package cream cheese, softened
- 1/2 cup sour cream
- 1/2 cup mayonnaise
- 1 cup shredded mozzarella cheese
- 1/2 cup grated Parmesan cheese
- 1/2 teaspoon garlic powder
- Salt and pepper, to taste
- Veggie sticks (carrots, celery, bell peppers) or chips, for serving

Instructions:

1. Preheat your oven to 375°F (190°C). Grease a baking dish (such as a 9-inch pie dish or small casserole dish).
2. Heat olive oil in a skillet over medium heat. Add chopped onion and cook until translucent, about 5 minutes.
3. Add minced garlic to the skillet and cook for another 1-2 minutes until fragrant.
4. Stir in thawed and drained chopped spinach and chopped artichoke hearts. Cook for 2-3 minutes until heated through.
5. In a large bowl, combine softened cream cheese, sour cream, mayonnaise, shredded mozzarella cheese, grated Parmesan cheese, garlic powder, salt, and pepper. Mix until smooth and well combined.
6. Add the cooked spinach and artichoke mixture to the bowl with the cheese mixture. Stir until evenly distributed.
7. Transfer the spinach and artichoke dip mixture to the greased baking dish, spreading it out evenly.
8. Bake in the preheated oven for 25-30 minutes, or until the dip is bubbly and the top is lightly golden brown.
9. Remove from the oven and let the dip cool for a few minutes before serving.
10. Serve the cheesy spinach and artichoke dip warm with veggie sticks (carrots, celery, bell peppers) or chips for dipping.

This Cheesy Spinach and Artichoke Dip is creamy, flavorful, and perfect for parties or gatherings. The combination of spinach, artichoke hearts, and cheesy goodness makes it a crowd-pleasing appetizer!

Veggie Loaded Baked Potatoes

Ingredients:

- 4 large baking potatoes (such as Russet or Idaho)
- Olive oil
- Salt and pepper, to taste
- 1 cup broccoli florets, steamed or roasted
- 1 cup cherry tomatoes, halved
- 1 cup corn kernels (fresh, frozen, or canned)
- 1/2 cup black beans, drained and rinsed
- 1/2 cup shredded cheddar cheese or Mexican blend cheese
- Sour cream or Greek yogurt, for topping
- Chopped green onions or chives, for garnish
- Salsa or hot sauce (optional)

Instructions:

1. Preheat your oven to 400°F (200°C).
2. Scrub the potatoes clean and pat them dry with a paper towel. Pierce each potato several times with a fork.
3. Rub the potatoes with olive oil and sprinkle with salt and pepper.
4. Place the potatoes directly on the oven rack or on a baking sheet lined with parchment paper. Bake for 45-60 minutes, or until the potatoes are tender when pierced with a fork.
5. While the potatoes are baking, prepare your toppings. Steam or roast the broccoli florets until tender-crisp. Halve the cherry tomatoes. Drain and rinse the black beans if using canned.
6. Once the potatoes are baked and tender, remove them from the oven and let them cool slightly.
7. Make a slit lengthwise in each potato and fluff the insides with a fork.
8. Top each potato with steamed or roasted broccoli florets, halved cherry tomatoes, corn kernels, and black beans.
9. Sprinkle shredded cheese over each loaded potato.
10. Return the loaded potatoes to the oven and bake for an additional 5-10 minutes, or until the cheese is melted and bubbly.
11. Remove from the oven and let the loaded baked potatoes cool for a few minutes.
12. Serve each loaded baked potato topped with a dollop of sour cream or Greek yogurt, chopped green onions or chives, and salsa or hot sauce if desired.

These Veggie Loaded Baked Potatoes are a hearty and satisfying meal. They're customizable with your favorite vegetables and toppings, making them a delicious option for lunch or dinner!

Broccoli and Cheese Casserole

Ingredients:

- 4 cups broccoli florets, blanched or steamed until tender-crisp
- 1 cup shredded cheddar cheese
- 1/2 cup grated Parmesan cheese
- 1/2 cup mayonnaise
- 1/2 cup sour cream
- 1 small onion, finely chopped
- 2 cloves garlic, minced
- 1/2 teaspoon salt, or to taste
- 1/4 teaspoon black pepper
- 1/4 teaspoon paprika
- 1/4 teaspoon dried thyme (optional)
- 1/2 cup breadcrumbs (panko or regular)
- 2 tablespoons melted butter
- Chopped fresh parsley, for garnish (optional)

Instructions:

1. Preheat your oven to 350°F (175°C). Grease a 9x13-inch baking dish.
2. In a large bowl, combine blanched or steamed broccoli florets, shredded cheddar cheese, grated Parmesan cheese, mayonnaise, sour cream, chopped onion, minced garlic, salt, pepper, paprika, and dried thyme. Mix until well combined.
3. Spread the broccoli mixture evenly into the prepared baking dish.
4. In a small bowl, mix together breadcrumbs and melted butter until well combined.
5. Sprinkle the breadcrumb mixture evenly over the top of the broccoli mixture.
6. Cover the baking dish with aluminum foil and bake in the preheated oven for 20 minutes.
7. Remove the foil and bake for an additional 10-15 minutes, or until the casserole is heated through and bubbly, and the breadcrumbs are golden brown.
8. Remove from the oven and let the casserole cool for a few minutes before serving.
9. Garnish with chopped fresh parsley, if desired, before serving.

This Broccoli and Cheese Casserole is creamy, cheesy, and packed with flavor. It's a perfect side dish for holidays, potlucks, or family dinners, and it's sure to be a hit with everyone at the table!

Butternut Squash Mac and Cheese

Ingredients:

- 1 medium butternut squash (about 2 pounds), peeled, seeded, and diced
- 1 tablespoon olive oil
- Salt and pepper, to taste
- 12 ounces elbow macaroni or pasta of your choice
- 2 tablespoons butter
- 2 tablespoons all-purpose flour
- 2 cups milk (preferably whole milk)
- 2 cups shredded sharp cheddar cheese
- 1/2 cup grated Parmesan cheese
- 1/2 teaspoon garlic powder
- 1/4 teaspoon ground nutmeg (optional)
- Fresh parsley, chopped, for garnish (optional)

Instructions:

1. Preheat your oven to 400°F (200°C).
2. Toss the diced butternut squash with olive oil, salt, and pepper. Spread evenly on a baking sheet lined with parchment paper.
3. Roast the butternut squash in the preheated oven for 20-25 minutes, or until tender and lightly caramelized. Remove from the oven and set aside.
4. While the butternut squash is roasting, cook the pasta in a large pot of salted boiling water according to package instructions until al dente. Drain and set aside.
5. In a large saucepan or skillet, melt the butter over medium heat. Stir in the flour and cook for 1-2 minutes until smooth and bubbly, stirring constantly.
6. Gradually whisk in the milk, stirring constantly to prevent lumps. Cook until the mixture thickens and comes to a simmer, about 5-7 minutes.
7. Remove the saucepan from heat and stir in the shredded cheddar cheese and grated Parmesan cheese until melted and smooth.
8. Add the roasted butternut squash to the cheese sauce, along with garlic powder and ground nutmeg (if using). Stir until well combined and smooth.
9. Add the cooked pasta to the sauce and gently toss until the pasta is evenly coated with the butternut squash cheese sauce.
10. Taste and adjust seasoning with salt and pepper, if needed.
11. Serve the Butternut Squash Mac and Cheese warm, garnished with chopped fresh parsley if desired.

This Butternut Squash Mac and Cheese is creamy, cheesy, and has a hint of sweetness from the roasted squash. It's a delightful twist on traditional mac and cheese, perfect for a cozy dinner or special occasion!

Veggie Pasta Salad

Ingredients:

- 8 ounces rotini or fusilli pasta (or any pasta shape of your choice)
- 1 cup cherry tomatoes, halved
- 1 cucumber, diced
- 1 bell pepper (any color), diced
- 1/2 red onion, thinly sliced
- 1/2 cup black olives, sliced
- 1/2 cup crumbled feta cheese (optional)
- 1/4 cup chopped fresh parsley or basil

For the dressing:

- 1/4 cup olive oil
- 2 tablespoons red wine vinegar or balsamic vinegar
- 1 clove garlic, minced
- 1 teaspoon Dijon mustard
- 1 teaspoon honey or maple syrup
- Salt and pepper, to taste

Instructions:

1. Cook the pasta according to package instructions in a large pot of salted boiling water until al dente. Drain and rinse under cold water to stop the cooking process. Let it cool completely.
2. In a large bowl, combine the cooled pasta, cherry tomatoes, cucumber, bell pepper, red onion, black olives, feta cheese (if using), and chopped fresh herbs.
3. In a small bowl or jar, whisk together the olive oil, red wine vinegar or balsamic vinegar, minced garlic, Dijon mustard, honey or maple syrup, salt, and pepper to make the dressing.
4. Pour the dressing over the pasta salad and toss gently to coat all ingredients evenly.
5. Taste and adjust seasoning with salt and pepper, if needed.
6. Cover the bowl with plastic wrap or transfer to an airtight container. Refrigerate for at least 1 hour before serving to allow the flavors to meld together.
7. Before serving, give the pasta salad a gentle toss. If needed, add a splash of olive oil or vinegar to refresh the salad.
8. Serve the Veggie Pasta Salad chilled or at room temperature, garnished with additional fresh herbs if desired.

This Veggie Pasta Salad is light, flavorful, and packed with colorful vegetables. It's versatile and can be customized with your favorite veggies or add-ins. Enjoy it as a side dish or a main meal for a refreshing and satisfying option!

Sweet Corn and Zucchini Pancakes

Ingredients:

- 1 cup grated zucchini (about 1 medium zucchini)
- 1 cup fresh or frozen sweet corn kernels (thawed if using frozen)
- 1/2 cup all-purpose flour
- 1/4 cup cornmeal
- 1/2 teaspoon baking powder
- 1/2 teaspoon baking soda
- 1/2 teaspoon salt
- 1/4 teaspoon black pepper
- 1/4 teaspoon paprika (optional)
- 2 green onions, thinly sliced
- 1/4 cup grated Parmesan cheese
- 2 large eggs, lightly beaten
- 1/4 cup milk
- Olive oil or cooking spray, for cooking

Instructions:

1. Grate the zucchini using a box grater. Place the grated zucchini in a clean kitchen towel or cheesecloth and squeeze out excess moisture. Transfer the squeezed zucchini to a large mixing bowl.
2. Add the sweet corn kernels, flour, cornmeal, baking powder, baking soda, salt, black pepper, paprika (if using), sliced green onions, and grated Parmesan cheese to the bowl with the zucchini. Mix well to combine.
3. In a separate bowl, whisk together the lightly beaten eggs and milk.
4. Pour the egg and milk mixture over the zucchini and corn mixture. Stir until all ingredients are well combined and a batter forms. The batter should be thick but pourable. If it's too thick, add a little more milk.
5. Heat a large skillet or griddle over medium heat. Brush with olive oil or coat with cooking spray.
6. Spoon about 1/4 cup of batter onto the skillet for each pancake, spreading it slightly with the back of a spoon to form a round shape.
7. Cook the pancakes for 3-4 minutes on each side, or until golden brown and cooked through. Flip carefully using a spatula.
8. Transfer cooked pancakes to a plate and cover loosely with foil to keep warm while you cook the remaining pancakes.
9. Serve the Sweet Corn and Zucchini Pancakes warm, topped with a dollop of sour cream, salsa, or your favorite sauce.

These Sweet Corn and Zucchini Pancakes are deliciously savory with a hint of sweetness from the corn. They're perfect for using up summer zucchini and corn, and they make a satisfying and flavorful meal any time of day!

Cheesy Polenta Fries

Ingredients:

- 1 cup polenta (cornmeal)
- 4 cups water
- 1 teaspoon salt
- 1 cup shredded cheddar cheese
- 1/4 cup grated Parmesan cheese
- 1/2 teaspoon garlic powder
- 1/2 teaspoon paprika
- Cooking spray or olive oil, for greasing

Instructions:

1. In a medium saucepan, bring 4 cups of water to a boil. Gradually whisk in the polenta and salt.
2. Reduce the heat to low and simmer, stirring frequently with a wooden spoon, for about 20-25 minutes or until the polenta is thick and creamy.
3. Remove the polenta from the heat and stir in the shredded cheddar cheese, grated Parmesan cheese, garlic powder, and paprika until well combined and the cheese is melted.
4. Line a baking sheet with parchment paper and lightly grease with cooking spray or olive oil.
5. Pour the cooked polenta onto the prepared baking sheet and spread it out evenly into a rectangle shape, about 1/2-inch thick.
6. Refrigerate the polenta for at least 1 hour or until completely cooled and firm.
7. Preheat your oven to 450°F (230°C).
8. Once chilled, use a sharp knife to cut the polenta into rectangular fries or wedges.
9. Arrange the polenta fries on the prepared baking sheet, leaving space between each fry.
10. Bake in the preheated oven for 20-25 minutes, flipping halfway through, or until the polenta fries are crispy and golden brown.
11. Remove from the oven and let them cool slightly before serving.
12. Serve the Cheesy Polenta Fries hot, optionally with a dipping sauce such as marinara sauce or a garlic aioli.

These Cheesy Polenta Fries are crispy on the outside and creamy on the inside with a delightful cheesy flavor. They make a fantastic appetizer or side dish that's sure to please both kids and adults alike!

Veggie Stuffed Mushrooms

Ingredients:

- 16 large white mushrooms
- 1 tablespoon olive oil
- 1 small onion, finely chopped
- 2 cloves garlic, minced
- 1/2 red bell pepper, finely chopped
- 1/2 yellow bell pepper, finely chopped
- 1/2 zucchini, finely chopped
- 1/2 cup cherry tomatoes, quartered
- 1/2 cup spinach, chopped
- 1/4 cup grated Parmesan cheese
- 1/4 cup breadcrumbs
- Salt and pepper, to taste
- Fresh parsley, chopped, for garnish

Instructions:

1. Preheat your oven to 375°F (190°C). Grease a baking sheet or line it with parchment paper.
2. Clean the mushrooms with a damp cloth to remove any dirt. Remove the stems and finely chop them. Set aside.
3. Heat olive oil in a large skillet over medium heat. Add chopped onion and cook until translucent, about 5 minutes.
4. Add minced garlic and chopped bell peppers to the skillet. Cook for another 2-3 minutes until bell peppers are slightly softened.
5. Stir in chopped zucchini and chopped mushroom stems. Cook for 3-4 minutes until vegetables are tender.
6. Add cherry tomatoes and chopped spinach to the skillet. Cook for another 2-3 minutes until spinach is wilted.
7. Remove the skillet from heat and stir in grated Parmesan cheese and breadcrumbs. Season with salt and pepper to taste.
8. Stuff each mushroom cap with the vegetable mixture, pressing gently to fill.
9. Place the stuffed mushrooms on the prepared baking sheet.
10. Bake in the preheated oven for 15-20 minutes, or until the mushrooms are tender and the filling is golden brown.
11. Remove from the oven and let the stuffed mushrooms cool for a few minutes before serving.
12. Garnish with chopped fresh parsley before serving.

These Veggie Stuffed Mushrooms are flavorful and nutritious, packed with a variety of vegetables and topped with a crispy breadcrumb and Parmesan cheese topping. They make a fantastic appetizer for parties or a delicious side dish for any meal!

Quinoa and Veggie Bowls

Ingredients:

- 1 cup quinoa, rinsed
- 2 cups water or vegetable broth
- 1 tablespoon olive oil
- 1 small onion, diced
- 2 cloves garlic, minced
- 1 bell pepper (any color), diced
- 1 zucchini, diced
- 1 cup cherry tomatoes, halved
- 1 cup cooked chickpeas (optional)
- 2 cups fresh spinach or kale, chopped
- Salt and pepper, to taste
- 1/4 cup chopped fresh herbs (such as parsley, cilantro, or basil)
- Lemon wedges, for serving

For the dressing (optional):

- 1/4 cup olive oil
- 2 tablespoons lemon juice
- 1 tablespoon balsamic vinegar or apple cider vinegar
- 1 teaspoon Dijon mustard
- 1 teaspoon honey or maple syrup
- Salt and pepper, to taste

Instructions:

1. In a medium saucepan, combine quinoa and water or vegetable broth. Bring to a boil over medium-high heat.
2. Reduce heat to low, cover, and simmer for 15-20 minutes, or until quinoa is cooked and liquid is absorbed. Remove from heat and let it sit covered for 5 minutes. Fluff with a fork.
3. While the quinoa is cooking, heat olive oil in a large skillet over medium heat. Add diced onion and cook until translucent, about 5 minutes.
4. Add minced garlic to the skillet and cook for another 1-2 minutes until fragrant.
5. Add diced bell pepper and zucchini to the skillet. Cook for 5-7 minutes until vegetables are tender-crisp.
6. Stir in halved cherry tomatoes and cooked chickpeas (if using). Cook for another 2-3 minutes until tomatoes are slightly softened.
7. Add chopped spinach or kale to the skillet and cook until wilted, about 2 minutes.
8. Season the vegetable mixture with salt and pepper to taste.
9. To assemble the bowls, divide cooked quinoa evenly among serving bowls. Top each bowl with the sautéed vegetable mixture.

10. If desired, drizzle each bowl with the prepared dressing (whisk together olive oil, lemon juice, balsamic or apple cider vinegar, Dijon mustard, honey or maple syrup, salt, and pepper).
11. Garnish each bowl with chopped fresh herbs and serve with lemon wedges on the side.

These Quinoa and Veggie Bowls are packed with protein, fiber, and vitamins from the quinoa and a variety of colorful vegetables. They're perfect for a healthy and satisfying lunch or dinner option that can be enjoyed warm or cold. Feel free to customize with your favorite veggies, beans, or additional toppings!

Veggie Meatballs with Marinara Sauce

Ingredients:

For the veggie meatballs:

- 1 cup cooked quinoa
- 1 cup cooked lentils (green or brown), mashed
- 1/2 cup grated zucchini, squeezed to remove excess moisture
- 1/2 cup grated carrots
- 1/4 cup finely chopped onion
- 2 cloves garlic, minced
- 1/4 cup chopped fresh parsley
- 1/4 cup grated Parmesan cheese (optional)
- 1/2 cup breadcrumbs (panko or regular)
- 2 tablespoons tomato paste
- 1 teaspoon dried oregano
- 1 teaspoon dried basil
- Salt and pepper, to taste
- Olive oil, for cooking

For the marinara sauce:

- 2 tablespoons olive oil
- 1 small onion, finely chopped
- 2 cloves garlic, minced
- 1 (28-ounce) can crushed tomatoes
- 1 teaspoon dried oregano
- 1 teaspoon dried basil
- Salt and pepper, to taste
- Fresh basil, chopped, for garnish (optional)

Instructions:

1. Prepare the veggie meatballs:
    - Preheat your oven to 375°F (190°C). Line a baking sheet with parchment paper.
    - In a large mixing bowl, combine cooked quinoa, mashed lentils, grated zucchini, grated carrots, chopped onion, minced garlic, chopped parsley, grated Parmesan cheese (if using), breadcrumbs, tomato paste, dried oregano, dried basil, salt, and pepper. Mix until well combined.
    - Roll the mixture into golf ball-sized balls and place them on the prepared baking sheet.
    - Brush or spray the veggie meatballs lightly with olive oil.
    - Bake in the preheated oven for 20-25 minutes, or until the meatballs are firm and golden brown.

2. Prepare the marinara sauce:
    - While the veggie meatballs are baking, heat olive oil in a large saucepan over medium heat.
    - Add finely chopped onion and cook until translucent, about 5 minutes.
    - Add minced garlic to the saucepan and cook for another 1-2 minutes until fragrant.
    - Stir in crushed tomatoes, dried oregano, dried basil, salt, and pepper. Bring the sauce to a simmer.
    - Reduce heat to low and let the sauce simmer for 15-20 minutes, stirring occasionally, to allow the flavors to meld together.
    - Taste and adjust seasoning with salt and pepper, if needed.
3. Assemble the dish:
    - Once the veggie meatballs are cooked and the marinara sauce is ready, gently add the meatballs to the saucepan with the marinara sauce.
    - Spoon some of the marinara sauce over the veggie meatballs to coat them evenly.
    - Serve the veggie meatballs with marinara sauce hot, garnished with chopped fresh basil if desired.

These Veggie Meatballs with Marinara Sauce are hearty, flavorful, and a great vegetarian alternative to traditional meatballs. They pair well with pasta, spaghetti squash, or even on their own with a side of crusty bread. Enjoy!

Spinach and Cheese Pinwheels

Ingredients:

- 1 sheet puff pastry, thawed according to package instructions
- 1 cup fresh spinach, chopped
- 1 cup shredded mozzarella cheese
- 1/4 cup grated Parmesan cheese
- 1 clove garlic, minced
- 1/2 teaspoon dried oregano
- Salt and pepper, to taste
- Olive oil or cooking spray, for brushing

Instructions:

1. Preheat your oven to 400°F (200°C). Line a baking sheet with parchment paper.
2. In a bowl, combine chopped spinach, shredded mozzarella cheese, grated Parmesan cheese, minced garlic, dried oregano, salt, and pepper. Mix well to combine.
3. Roll out the thawed puff pastry sheet on a lightly floured surface into a rectangle.
4. Spread the spinach and cheese mixture evenly over the puff pastry sheet, leaving a small border along the edges.
5. Starting from one of the longer edges, tightly roll up the puff pastry sheet into a log.
6. Using a sharp knife, slice the log into 1-inch thick rounds.
7. Place the pinwheels on the prepared baking sheet, cut side down, spacing them slightly apart.
8. Brush the tops of the pinwheels lightly with olive oil or spray with cooking spray.
9. Bake in the preheated oven for 15-18 minutes, or until the pinwheels are golden brown and puffed up.
10. Remove from the oven and let cool slightly before serving.

These Spinach and Cheese Pinwheels are crispy on the outside and filled with a savory spinach and cheese filling. They make a great appetizer for parties or a delicious snack any time of the day!

Baked Falafel with Cucumber Yogurt Dip

Ingredients:

For the falafel:

- 1 can (15 oz) chickpeas, drained and rinsed
- 1/2 cup fresh parsley, chopped
- 1/2 cup fresh cilantro, chopped
- 3 cloves garlic, minced
- 1 small onion, chopped
- 1 teaspoon ground cumin
- 1 teaspoon ground coriander
- 1/2 teaspoon paprika
- 1/4 teaspoon cayenne pepper (optional, for heat)
- 1 tablespoon lemon juice
- 1 tablespoon olive oil
- 1/2 teaspoon salt
- 1/4 teaspoon black pepper
- 1/2 teaspoon baking powder
- 1/4 cup breadcrumbs (panko or regular)
- Olive oil or cooking spray, for brushing

For the cucumber yogurt dip:

- 1 cup plain Greek yogurt
- 1/2 cucumber, grated and excess moisture squeezed out
- 1 clove garlic, minced
- 1 tablespoon lemon juice
- 1 tablespoon chopped fresh dill (or 1 teaspoon dried dill)
- Salt and pepper, to taste

Instructions:

1. Prepare the falafel:
    - Preheat your oven to 375°F (190°C). Line a baking sheet with parchment paper.
    - In a food processor, combine chickpeas, chopped parsley, chopped cilantro, minced garlic, chopped onion, ground cumin, ground coriander, paprika, cayenne pepper (if using), lemon juice, olive oil, salt, and black pepper. Pulse until the mixture is well combined and forms a coarse paste.
    - Transfer the falafel mixture to a mixing bowl. Stir in baking powder and breadcrumbs until evenly incorporated.
    - Shape the falafel mixture into small patties or balls and place them on the prepared baking sheet.
    - Brush the tops of the falafel with olive oil or spray lightly with cooking spray.

- Bake in the preheated oven for 20-25 minutes, flipping halfway through, or until the falafel is golden brown and crispy.
2. Prepare the cucumber yogurt dip:
    - In a small bowl, combine plain Greek yogurt, grated cucumber, minced garlic, lemon juice, chopped fresh dill (or dried dill), salt, and pepper. Mix until well combined.
    - Taste and adjust seasoning with additional salt, pepper, or lemon juice if desired.
3. Serve:
    - Serve the baked falafel warm with the cucumber yogurt dip on the side.
    - Optionally, serve with pita bread, sliced vegetables, or a salad.

This Baked Falafel with Cucumber Yogurt Dip is a healthier twist on the traditional fried falafel, with a fresh and tangy dip that complements the crispy falafel perfectly. Enjoy this dish as a main meal or as a delightful appetizer!

Veggie-Packed Minestrone Soup

Ingredients:

- 2 tablespoons olive oil
- 1 onion, diced
- 2 carrots, diced
- 2 celery stalks, diced
- 3 cloves garlic, minced
- 1 zucchini, diced
- 1 yellow squash, diced
- 1 cup green beans, trimmed and cut into 1-inch pieces
- 1 can (15 oz) diced tomatoes
- 1 can (15 oz) kidney beans, drained and rinsed
- 6 cups vegetable broth
- 1 teaspoon dried oregano
- 1 teaspoon dried basil
- 1 teaspoon dried thyme
- Salt and pepper, to taste
- 1 cup small pasta (such as ditalini or small shells)
- 2 cups fresh spinach or kale, chopped
- Grated Parmesan cheese, for serving (optional)
- Fresh basil or parsley, chopped, for garnish (optional)

Instructions:

1. In a large pot or Dutch oven, heat olive oil over medium heat. Add diced onion, carrots, and celery. Cook for 5-7 minutes, or until vegetables are softened and onions are translucent.
2. Add minced garlic and cook for another 1-2 minutes until fragrant.
3. Stir in diced zucchini, yellow squash, and green beans. Cook for 5 minutes, stirring occasionally.
4. Add diced tomatoes (with juices), kidney beans, vegetable broth, dried oregano, dried basil, dried thyme, salt, and pepper to the pot. Bring to a boil.
5. Once boiling, reduce heat to low and let the soup simmer uncovered for 20-25 minutes, or until the vegetables are tender.
6. Stir in small pasta and continue to simmer for 10-12 minutes, or until the pasta is cooked al dente.
7. Add chopped spinach or kale to the soup and cook for another 1-2 minutes until wilted.
8. Taste and adjust seasoning with salt and pepper if needed.
9. Remove the soup from heat. Serve hot, garnished with grated Parmesan cheese and chopped fresh basil or parsley if desired.
10. Enjoy this hearty and veggie-packed Minestrone Soup as a comforting meal. It's even better the next day as flavors continue to meld together!

This Veggie-Packed Minestrone Soup is not only delicious but also versatile. Feel free to customize it with your favorite vegetables or add beans like cannellini beans for additional protein. It's perfect for chilly days and makes for a satisfying and nutritious meal.

Veggie Empanadas

Ingredients:

For the dough:

- 2 cups all-purpose flour
- 1 teaspoon salt
- 1/2 cup unsalted butter, chilled and cut into small cubes
- 1/2 cup cold water

For the filling:

- 1 tablespoon olive oil
- 1 small onion, finely chopped
- 2 cloves garlic, minced
- 1 red bell pepper, diced
- 1 green bell pepper, diced
- 1 zucchini, diced
- 1 cup corn kernels (fresh or frozen)
- 1 cup black beans, cooked and drained
- 1 teaspoon ground cumin
- 1 teaspoon paprika
- 1/2 teaspoon chili powder (optional)
- Salt and pepper, to taste
- 1/4 cup chopped fresh cilantro or parsley
- 1/2 cup shredded cheese (cheddar, mozzarella, or your choice)
- Egg wash (1 egg beaten with 1 tablespoon water), for brushing

Instructions:

1. Prepare the dough:
    - In a large bowl, whisk together flour and salt. Add chilled butter cubes and use your fingers or a pastry cutter to work the butter into the flour until it resembles coarse crumbs.
    - Gradually add cold water, a tablespoon at a time, mixing with a fork until the dough comes together and forms a ball.
    - Wrap the dough in plastic wrap and refrigerate for at least 30 minutes while you prepare the filling.
2. Prepare the filling:
    - Heat olive oil in a large skillet over medium heat. Add chopped onion and cook until translucent, about 5 minutes.
    - Add minced garlic and diced bell peppers to the skillet. Cook for another 3-4 minutes until peppers are slightly softened.

- Stir in diced zucchini, corn kernels, and black beans. Cook for 5-7 minutes, stirring occasionally, until vegetables are tender.
- Add ground cumin, paprika, chili powder (if using), salt, and pepper to the skillet. Stir to combine and cook for another minute.
- Remove from heat and stir in chopped fresh cilantro or parsley. Let the filling cool slightly.

3. Assemble the empanadas:
    - Preheat your oven to 375°F (190°C). Line a baking sheet with parchment paper.
    - On a lightly floured surface, roll out the chilled dough to about 1/8-inch thickness. Use a round cutter (about 5 inches in diameter) to cut out circles of dough.
    - Place a spoonful of the vegetable filling on one half of each dough circle, leaving a small border around the edges. Top with shredded cheese.
    - Fold the dough over the filling to create a half-moon shape. Press the edges together with your fingers or use a fork to crimp and seal the edges.
    - Place the assembled empanadas on the prepared baking sheet. Brush the tops with egg wash for a golden finish.
4. Bake the empanadas:
    - Bake in the preheated oven for 20-25 minutes, or until the empanadas are golden brown and crispy.
    - Remove from the oven and let them cool slightly before serving.
5. Serve:
    - Serve the Veggie Empanadas warm as a delicious appetizer, snack, or light meal. They can be enjoyed on their own or with a side of salsa, guacamole, or sour cream for dipping.

These Veggie Empanadas are filled with a flavorful and nutritious vegetable mixture wrapped in a buttery, flaky pastry crust. They're perfect for sharing with family and friends or enjoying as a satisfying meal!

Spinach and Ricotta Stuffed Manicotti

Ingredients:

For the manicotti:

- 1 box (8 oz) manicotti shells
- 1 tablespoon olive oil
- 1 small onion, finely chopped
- 2 cloves garlic, minced
- 1 (10 oz) package frozen chopped spinach, thawed and drained
- 1 container (15 oz) ricotta cheese
- 1 cup shredded mozzarella cheese, divided
- 1/2 cup grated Parmesan cheese, divided
- 1 egg
- 1 teaspoon dried basil
- 1 teaspoon dried oregano
- Salt and pepper, to taste

For the marinara sauce:

- 1 tablespoon olive oil
- 1 small onion, finely chopped
- 2 cloves garlic, minced
- 1 (28 oz) can crushed tomatoes
- 1 teaspoon dried basil
- 1 teaspoon dried oregano
- Salt and pepper, to taste
- Fresh basil, chopped, for garnish (optional)

Instructions:

1. Cook the manicotti shells:
    - Preheat your oven to 350°F (175°C).
    - Cook manicotti shells according to package instructions until al dente. Drain and rinse with cold water to stop the cooking process. Set aside.
2. Prepare the filling:
    - Heat olive oil in a large skillet over medium heat. Add chopped onion and cook until translucent, about 5 minutes.
    - Add minced garlic and cook for another 1-2 minutes until fragrant.
    - Stir in thawed and drained spinach and cook for 2-3 minutes to remove excess moisture.
    - In a large mixing bowl, combine ricotta cheese, 1/2 cup shredded mozzarella cheese, 1/4 cup grated Parmesan cheese, egg, dried basil, dried oregano, salt, and pepper. Mix well.

- Add the spinach mixture to the ricotta mixture and stir until evenly combined.
3. Fill the manicotti shells:
    - Spoon the spinach and ricotta mixture into a piping bag or a resealable plastic bag with a corner snipped off.
    - Pipe the filling into each manicotti shell until they are filled and plump.
4. Prepare the marinara sauce:
    - In the same skillet used for the filling, heat olive oil over medium heat. Add chopped onion and cook until translucent, about 5 minutes.
    - Add minced garlic and cook for another 1-2 minutes until fragrant.
    - Stir in crushed tomatoes, dried basil, dried oregano, salt, and pepper. Bring to a simmer and cook for 10-15 minutes, stirring occasionally, to allow flavors to meld.
5. Assemble and bake:
    - Spread a thin layer of marinara sauce on the bottom of a 9x13-inch baking dish.
    - Arrange the filled manicotti shells in a single layer over the marinara sauce.
    - Pour the remaining marinara sauce over the manicotti shells, covering them completely.
    - Sprinkle the remaining 1/2 cup shredded mozzarella cheese and 1/4 cup grated Parmesan cheese over the top.
6. Bake:
    - Cover the baking dish with aluminum foil and bake in the preheated oven for 25-30 minutes.
    - Remove the foil and bake for an additional 10-15 minutes, or until the cheese is melted and bubbly.
7. Serve:
    - Remove from the oven and let the Spinach and Ricotta Stuffed Manicotti cool for a few minutes before serving.
    - Garnish with chopped fresh basil if desired.

Enjoy this comforting and cheesy Spinach and Ricotta Stuffed Manicotti with a side salad and garlic bread for a delicious Italian-inspired meal!

Black Bean and Corn Tacos

Ingredients:

- 1 tablespoon olive oil
- 1 small onion, diced
- 2 cloves garlic, minced
- 1 red bell pepper, diced
- 1 jalapeño, seeded and finely chopped (optional, for heat)
- 1 teaspoon ground cumin
- 1 teaspoon chili powder
- 1 can (15 oz) black beans, drained and rinsed
- 1 cup frozen corn kernels
- Salt and pepper, to taste
- Juice of 1 lime
- 8 small corn or flour tortillas
- Toppings: shredded lettuce, diced tomatoes, diced avocado, salsa, cilantro, sour cream, etc.

Instructions:

1. Prepare the filling:
   - Heat olive oil in a large skillet over medium heat. Add diced onion and cook until translucent, about 5 minutes.
   - Add minced garlic and diced red bell pepper (and jalapeño if using). Cook for another 2-3 minutes until peppers are slightly softened.
   - Stir in ground cumin and chili powder, and cook for 1 minute until fragrant.
   - Add black beans and frozen corn kernels to the skillet. Cook for 5-7 minutes, stirring occasionally, until heated through.
   - Season with salt, pepper, and lime juice. Taste and adjust seasoning as needed.
2. Warm the tortillas:
   - While the filling is cooking, heat tortillas in a dry skillet over medium heat for about 30 seconds per side, or wrap them in a damp paper towel and microwave for 20-30 seconds until warm and pliable.
3. Assemble the tacos:
   - Spoon the black bean and corn mixture into warm tortillas.
   - Top with shredded lettuce, diced tomatoes, diced avocado, salsa, cilantro, sour cream, or your favorite taco toppings.
4. Serve:
   - Serve the Black Bean and Corn Tacos immediately while warm.
   - Enjoy these delicious and flavorful tacos as a quick and satisfying meal!

These Black Bean and Corn Tacos are versatile and can be customized with your favorite toppings and additions like cheese or hot sauce. They're perfect for a meatless meal that's packed with protein and flavor.

Ratatouille

Ingredients:

- 1 large eggplant, diced into 1-inch cubes
- 2 zucchinis, diced into 1-inch cubes
- 1 yellow bell pepper, diced
- 1 red bell pepper, diced
- 1 onion, diced
- 3 cloves garlic, minced
- 2 tomatoes, diced
- 1 can (15 oz) crushed tomatoes
- 2 tablespoons tomato paste
- 2 tablespoons olive oil
- 1 teaspoon dried thyme
- 1 teaspoon dried oregano
- Salt and pepper, to taste
- Fresh basil or parsley, chopped, for garnish

Instructions:

1. Prepare the vegetables:
    - Heat 1 tablespoon of olive oil in a large skillet or Dutch oven over medium-high heat.
    - Add diced eggplant and cook until lightly browned and softened, about 5-7 minutes. Remove from the skillet and set aside.
    - Add another tablespoon of olive oil to the skillet. Add diced zucchini and bell peppers. Cook for 5 minutes until softened. Remove and set aside with the eggplant.
2. Make the stew:
    - In the same skillet, add diced onion and cook until translucent, about 5 minutes.
    - Add minced garlic and cook for another 1-2 minutes until fragrant.
    - Stir in diced tomatoes, crushed tomatoes, and tomato paste. Bring to a simmer.
    - Add dried thyme, dried oregano, salt, and pepper to taste. Stir well to combine.
    - Return cooked eggplant, zucchini, and bell peppers to the skillet. Stir gently to combine all ingredients.
3. Simmer:
    - Reduce heat to low and let the ratatouille simmer gently for 20-30 minutes, stirring occasionally, until the vegetables are tender and the flavors have melded together.
4. Serve:
    - Remove from heat and taste for seasoning. Adjust salt and pepper if needed.
    - Serve ratatouille hot, garnished with chopped fresh basil or parsley.
    - Enjoy as a main dish with crusty bread or as a side dish to grilled meats or fish.

Ratatouille can be enjoyed immediately, but it's even better the next day when the flavors have had time to develop. It's a versatile dish that can be served hot, cold, or at room temperature, making it perfect for any season.

Vegetable Fried Rice

Ingredients:

- 2 cups cooked rice (preferably chilled, day-old rice works best)
- 2 tablespoons sesame oil (or vegetable oil)
- 2 cloves garlic, minced
- 1 small onion, diced
- 1 carrot, diced
- 1 bell pepper (any color), diced
- 1 cup frozen peas and carrots mix (or any frozen vegetables of your choice)
- 2-3 tablespoons soy sauce (adjust to taste)
- 1 tablespoon oyster sauce (optional)
- 2 eggs, lightly beaten
- Salt and pepper, to taste
- Green onions, chopped (for garnish)
- Sesame seeds, for garnish (optional)

Instructions:

1. Prepare the rice:
    - If you haven't already cooked the rice, cook it according to package instructions and let it cool. Chilled rice works best for fried rice as it is less sticky.
2. Heat the oil:
    - Heat sesame oil (or vegetable oil) in a large skillet or wok over medium-high heat.
3. Cook the aromatics:
    - Add minced garlic and diced onion to the skillet. Stir-fry for 1-2 minutes until fragrant and onions are translucent.
4. Add the vegetables:
    - Add diced carrot, bell pepper, and frozen peas and carrots mix (or other frozen vegetables). Stir-fry for 3-4 minutes until vegetables are tender-crisp.
5. Push vegetables to the side:
    - Push the vegetables to one side of the skillet. Pour the lightly beaten eggs into the empty space. Let them cook undisturbed for a few seconds until they start to set.
6. Scramble the eggs:
    - Use a spatula to scramble the eggs until they are cooked through but still slightly moist.
7. Combine everything:
    - Add the cooked rice to the skillet. Use a spatula to break up any clumps of rice and mix everything together.
8. Season the fried rice:
    - Drizzle soy sauce and oyster sauce (if using) over the rice. Stir well to coat all the rice and vegetables. Taste and adjust seasoning with salt and pepper as needed.

9. Finish and serve:
    - Remove from heat and garnish with chopped green onions and sesame seeds (if using).
    - Serve hot as a main dish or side dish. Enjoy your homemade Vegetable Fried Rice!

This recipe is versatile, so feel free to customize it by adding other vegetables like mushrooms, broccoli, or baby corn. You can also add protein such as cooked chicken, shrimp, or tofu for a more substantial meal.

Lentil Sloppy Joes

Ingredients:

- 1 cup brown or green lentils, rinsed
- 3 cups vegetable broth or water
- 1 tablespoon olive oil
- 1 onion, diced
- 1 bell pepper (any color), diced
- 2 cloves garlic, minced
- 1 can (15 oz) tomato sauce
- 2 tablespoons tomato paste
- 2 tablespoons soy sauce or tamari
- 1 tablespoon apple cider vinegar
- 1 tablespoon maple syrup or brown sugar
- 1 teaspoon chili powder
- 1/2 teaspoon smoked paprika
- Salt and pepper, to taste
- Hamburger buns or sandwich rolls, for serving

Instructions:

1. Cook the lentils:
   - In a medium saucepan, combine rinsed lentils and vegetable broth (or water). Bring to a boil, then reduce heat to low and simmer for 20-25 minutes, or until lentils are tender and most of the liquid is absorbed. Drain any excess liquid and set aside.
2. Prepare the sauce:
   - In a large skillet or saucepan, heat olive oil over medium heat. Add diced onion and bell pepper. Cook for 5-7 minutes, or until vegetables are softened.
3. Add seasonings:
   - Stir in minced garlic, chili powder, and smoked paprika. Cook for another 1-2 minutes until fragrant.
4. Combine sauce ingredients:
   - Add tomato sauce, tomato paste, soy sauce (or tamari), apple cider vinegar, maple syrup (or brown sugar), salt, and pepper to the skillet. Stir well to combine.
5. Simmer:
   - Add the cooked lentils to the skillet with the sauce. Stir to coat the lentils evenly with the sauce.
   - Reduce heat to low and simmer for 10-15 minutes, stirring occasionally, to allow flavors to meld together and the mixture to thicken.
6. Serve:
   - Toast the hamburger buns or sandwich rolls if desired.
   - Spoon the lentil mixture onto the bottom half of each bun.
   - Top with the other half of the bun and serve immediately.

7. Enjoy:
    - Serve Lentil Sloppy Joes with your favorite side dishes like coleslaw, potato chips, or a salad.
    - These sandwiches are deliciously satisfying, packed with protein and flavor!

This Lentil Sloppy Joes recipe is perfect for a quick and comforting meal, and it's a great way to enjoy a meatless version of a classic favorite. Adjust the seasonings to your taste and enjoy!

Veggie Stuffed Pita Pockets

Ingredients:

- 4 whole wheat pita pockets
- 1 cup hummus (store-bought or homemade)
- 1 cucumber, thinly sliced
- 1 bell pepper (any color), thinly sliced
- 1 cup cherry tomatoes, halved
- 1/2 red onion, thinly sliced
- 1 cup mixed greens (such as lettuce or spinach)
- Optional toppings: olives, feta cheese, avocado slices, sprouts, etc.
- Salt and pepper, to taste
- Fresh lemon juice (optional)

Instructions:

1. Prepare the pita pockets:
    - Warm the pita pockets in a toaster oven or microwave for a few seconds until they are soft and pliable.
2. Spread hummus:
    - Carefully open each pita pocket and spread about 1/4 cup of hummus inside each pocket.
3. Fill with veggies:
    - Stuff the pita pockets with cucumber slices, bell pepper slices, cherry tomatoes, red onion slices, and mixed greens. Add any optional toppings you desire.
4. Season and serve:
    - Season the filled pita pockets with salt, pepper, and a squeeze of fresh lemon juice if desired.
    - Serve immediately and enjoy your Veggie Stuffed Pita Pockets as a nutritious and delicious meal!

Variations:

- Protein Boost: Add grilled chicken, chickpeas, or tofu for extra protein.
- Mediterranean Twist: Add olives, feta cheese, and a drizzle of olive oil for a Mediterranean flavor.
- Spicy Kick: Add sliced jalapeños or a dash of hot sauce for some heat.

These Veggie Stuffed Pita Pockets are versatile and can be customized with your favorite vegetables and toppings. They're perfect for a quick lunch, dinner, or even a portable snack. Enjoy the freshness and flavors packed into each bite!

Grilled Veggie Sandwiches

Ingredients:

- 1 zucchini, sliced lengthwise
- 1 yellow squash, sliced lengthwise
- 1 red bell pepper, halved and deseeded
- 1 red onion, sliced into rings
- 1 eggplant, sliced into rounds
- 4 tablespoons olive oil
- Salt and pepper, to taste
- 8 slices of bread (whole grain or your choice)
- 1/2 cup hummus (store-bought or homemade)
- Handful of baby spinach or arugula
- Optional: sliced avocado, sprouts, or any other preferred sandwich toppings

Instructions:

1. Prepare the vegetables:
    - Preheat your grill or grill pan over medium-high heat.
    - Brush zucchini, yellow squash, red bell pepper, red onion, and eggplant slices with olive oil. Season with salt and pepper.
2. Grill the vegetables:
    - Grill the vegetables in batches until they are tender and have nice grill marks, about 3-4 minutes per side for the zucchini, yellow squash, red bell pepper, and eggplant. The red onion slices may take a little longer, about 5-6 minutes per side.
    - Remove the grilled vegetables from the grill and set aside.
3. Assemble the sandwiches:
    - Spread hummus evenly on each slice of bread.
    - Layer grilled vegetables on half of the bread slices.
    - Top with baby spinach or arugula and any additional toppings like avocado slices or sprouts.
4. Grill the sandwiches (optional):
    - If you prefer a warm sandwich, you can grill the assembled sandwiches on a grill pan or in a panini press for a few minutes until the bread is toasted and golden brown.
5. Serve:
    - Cut the grilled veggie sandwiches in half diagonally and serve immediately.

Tips:

- Variety of Vegetables: Feel free to use any seasonal vegetables you have on hand or prefer.

- Bread Options: Experiment with different types of bread such as ciabatta, whole grain, or sourdough.
- Additional Flavors: Enhance the sandwiches with a drizzle of balsamic glaze, a sprinkle of feta cheese, or a dollop of pesto for added flavor.

These Grilled Veggie Sandwiches are nutritious, packed with flavor, and perfect for a satisfying lunch or dinner option. Enjoy the combination of grilled vegetables, creamy hummus, and fresh greens for a delightful meal!

Veggie-Packed Chili

Ingredients:

- 1 tablespoon olive oil
- 1 onion, diced
- 3 cloves garlic, minced
- 1 red bell pepper, diced
- 1 green bell pepper, diced
- 2 carrots, diced
- 2 celery stalks, diced
- 1 zucchini, diced
- 1 yellow squash, diced
- 1 jalapeño pepper, seeded and finely chopped (optional, for heat)
- 1 can (15 oz) black beans, drained and rinsed
- 1 can (15 oz) kidney beans, drained and rinsed
- 1 can (15 oz) diced tomatoes
- 1 can (15 oz) tomato sauce
- 1 cup vegetable broth or water
- 2 tablespoons chili powder
- 1 tablespoon ground cumin
- 1 teaspoon paprika
- Salt and pepper, to taste
- Optional toppings: shredded cheese, sour cream, chopped cilantro, avocado slices, diced green onions

Instructions:

1. Sauté vegetables:
   - Heat olive oil in a large pot or Dutch oven over medium heat. Add diced onion and garlic. Sauté for 3-4 minutes until onions are translucent and garlic is fragrant.
2. Add bell peppers, carrots, and celery:
   - Add diced red and green bell peppers, carrots, and celery to the pot. Cook for 5-7 minutes, stirring occasionally, until vegetables begin to soften.
3. Add zucchini, yellow squash, and jalapeño (if using):
   - Stir in diced zucchini, yellow squash, and jalapeño pepper. Cook for another 3-4 minutes.
4. Add beans and tomatoes:
   - Add drained and rinsed black beans and kidney beans to the pot. Stir in diced tomatoes and tomato sauce.
5. Season and simmer:
   - Stir in chili powder, ground cumin, paprika, salt, and pepper. Pour in vegetable broth or water. Bring the chili to a simmer.
6. Simmer and cook:

- - Reduce heat to low and let the chili simmer uncovered for 30-40 minutes, stirring occasionally, until flavors are well blended and vegetables are tender.
7. Adjust seasoning:
    - Taste and adjust seasoning with more salt, pepper, or chili powder if needed.
8. Serve:
    - Ladle the veggie-packed chili into bowls. Serve hot with optional toppings such as shredded cheese, sour cream, chopped cilantro, avocado slices, or diced green onions.

Tips:

- Texture and Thickness: For a thicker chili, you can mash some of the beans with a fork or blend a small portion of the chili with an immersion blender.
- Make it Spicy: Adjust the heat level by adding more jalapeño peppers or a dash of hot sauce.
- Storage: This chili freezes well. Cool completely before storing in airtight containers in the refrigerator for up to 5 days or in the freezer for up to 3 months.

Enjoy this hearty and veggie-packed chili as a comforting meal that's full of flavors and nutrients!

Sweet Potato and Black Bean Enchiladas

Here's a delicious recipe for Sweet Potato and Black Bean Enchiladas, combining hearty sweet potatoes with savory black beans and flavorful enchilada sauce:

Sweet Potato and Black Bean Enchiladas

Ingredients:

- 2 medium sweet potatoes, peeled and diced
- 1 tablespoon olive oil
- 1 onion, diced
- 2 cloves garlic, minced
- 1 red bell pepper, diced
- 1 jalapeño pepper, seeded and finely chopped (optional, for heat)
- 1 can (15 oz) black beans, drained and rinsed
- 1 teaspoon ground cumin
- 1 teaspoon chili powder
- 1/2 teaspoon smoked paprika
- Salt and pepper, to taste
- 1 can (15 oz) red enchilada sauce
- 8-10 small flour or corn tortillas
- 1 cup shredded cheese (cheddar, Monterey Jack, or a blend)
- Fresh cilantro, chopped, for garnish
- Optional toppings: sour cream, avocado slices, diced tomatoes, sliced green onions

Instructions:

1. Prepare the sweet potatoes:
   - Preheat your oven to 400°F (200°C).
   - Toss diced sweet potatoes with olive oil, salt, and pepper. Spread them out on a baking sheet lined with parchment paper.
   - Roast in the preheated oven for 20-25 minutes, or until tender and lightly browned. Remove from the oven and set aside.
2. Prepare the filling:
   - In a large skillet, heat olive oil over medium heat. Add diced onion and cook until translucent, about 5 minutes.
   - Add minced garlic, diced red bell pepper, and jalapeño pepper (if using). Cook for another 2-3 minutes until peppers are softened.
3. Combine with black beans and spices:
   - Stir in drained and rinsed black beans, ground cumin, chili powder, smoked paprika, salt, and pepper. Cook for 2-3 minutes to allow flavors to meld. Remove from heat.
4. Assemble the enchiladas:
   - Spread a thin layer of enchilada sauce on the bottom of a 9x13-inch baking dish.
   - Warm tortillas in the microwave for a few seconds to make them pliable. Place a spoonful of the sweet potato mixture and black bean mixture in the center of each tortilla. Roll up tightly and place seam side down in the baking dish.
5. Cover with sauce and cheese:

- Pour the remaining enchilada sauce over the assembled enchiladas, spreading it evenly to cover them.
    - Sprinkle shredded cheese over the top of the enchiladas.
6. Bake:
    - Cover the baking dish with aluminum foil and bake in the preheated oven for 20-25 minutes, until the enchiladas are heated through and the cheese is melted and bubbly.
7. Serve:
    - Remove from the oven and let cool slightly. Garnish with chopped fresh cilantro and serve with optional toppings such as sour cream, avocado slices, diced tomatoes, or sliced green onions.

Tips:

- Make it Vegan: Use dairy-free cheese or skip the cheese altogether.
- Customize: Add spinach or corn to the filling for extra flavor and nutrition.
- Prepare Ahead: You can assemble the enchiladas ahead of time and refrigerate them until ready to bake.

These Sweet Potato and Black Bean Enchiladas are packed with flavor and nutrients, making them a satisfying meal for both vegetarians and meat-eaters alike! Enjoy the delicious combination of sweet potatoes, black beans, and spices wrapped in a warm tortilla with your favorite toppings.

Baked Veggie Spring Rolls

Ingredients:

- 1 package (about 10-12) spring roll wrappers (available in Asian grocery stores or the international aisle of supermarkets)
- 2 cups finely shredded cabbage (green or napa cabbage)
- 1 carrot, julienned or grated
- 1 red bell pepper, thinly sliced
- 1 cup bean sprouts
- 3-4 green onions, thinly sliced
- 1 tablespoon soy sauce or tamari
- 1 tablespoon hoisin sauce
- 1 teaspoon sesame oil
- 1 teaspoon grated fresh ginger
- 1 clove garlic, minced
- Salt and pepper, to taste
- 2 tablespoons cornstarch mixed with 3 tablespoons water (for sealing rolls)
- Cooking spray or olive oil spray

Instructions:

1. Prepare the filling:
    - In a large bowl, combine shredded cabbage, julienned carrot, sliced bell pepper, bean sprouts, and green onions.
    - In a small bowl, mix together soy sauce (or tamari), hoisin sauce, sesame oil, grated ginger, minced garlic, salt, and pepper. Pour over the vegetables and toss to combine.
2. Prepare the spring roll wrappers:
    - Place one spring roll wrapper on a clean surface, with one corner pointing towards you (diamond shape). Keep the remaining wrappers covered with a damp towel to prevent drying out.
3. Fill and roll the spring rolls:
    - Spoon about 2-3 tablespoons of the vegetable filling onto the lower third of the wrapper, leaving a border on each side. Fold the bottom corner over the filling, then fold in the sides. Roll tightly upwards to seal. Brush the edges with the cornstarch-water mixture to secure the seal.
4. Bake the spring rolls:
    - Preheat the oven to 400°F (200°C). Line a baking sheet with parchment paper and lightly spray with cooking spray or brush with olive oil.
    - Place the rolled spring rolls seam side down on the baking sheet. Lightly spray the tops of the spring rolls with cooking spray or brush with olive oil.
    - Bake for 15-20 minutes, or until the spring rolls are golden brown and crispy, turning halfway through baking for even browning.
5. Serve:

- Remove from the oven and let cool slightly. Serve the baked veggie spring rolls warm with your favorite dipping sauce, such as sweet chili sauce, soy sauce, or hoisin sauce.

Tips:

- Variations: You can add cooked and shredded chicken, shrimp, or tofu to the vegetable filling for added protein.
- Storage: Baked spring rolls are best enjoyed fresh and crispy. If you have leftovers, store them in an airtight container in the refrigerator and reheat in the oven to crisp them up again.

These Baked Veggie Spring Rolls are a healthier alternative to fried versions, offering a crunchy exterior and a flavorful, vegetable-packed filling. They make a great appetizer, snack, or even a light meal when paired with a side salad. Enjoy making and eating these delicious treats!

Avocado and Veggie Sushi Bowls

Ingredients:

- 1 cup sushi rice, rinsed
- 1 1/4 cups water
- 1 tablespoon rice vinegar
- 1 tablespoon sugar
- 1/2 teaspoon salt
- 1 avocado, thinly sliced
- 1 cucumber, julienned or thinly sliced
- 1 carrot, julienned or grated
- 1/2 red bell pepper, thinly sliced
- 1/2 cup edamame, cooked and shelled
- 1 nori sheet, cut into thin strips or crumbled (optional)
- Sesame seeds, for garnish
- Pickled ginger, for serving (optional)
- Soy sauce or tamari, for serving

Instructions:

1. Cook the sushi rice:
    - In a medium saucepan, combine rinsed sushi rice and water. Bring to a boil, then reduce heat to low, cover, and simmer for 15-20 minutes, or until water is absorbed and rice is tender.
    - In a small bowl, mix rice vinegar, sugar, and salt until dissolved. Stir the vinegar mixture into the cooked rice and let it cool to room temperature.
2. Prepare the bowls:
    - Divide the sushi rice evenly among serving bowls.
    - Arrange avocado slices, julienned cucumber, julienned carrot, thinly sliced red bell pepper, and edamame on top of the rice in each bowl.
3. Garnish:
    - Sprinkle nori strips or crumbled nori over the bowls for added flavor and texture.
    - Sprinkle sesame seeds over the bowls for garnish.
4. Serve:
    - Serve the Avocado and Veggie Sushi Bowls immediately, with pickled ginger and soy sauce or tamari on the side.

Tips:

- Customize: Feel free to add other vegetables such as radishes, spinach, or sprouts according to your preference.
- Protein Boost: Add cooked shrimp, crab meat, or tofu cubes for additional protein.
- Make-Ahead: Prepare the components ahead of time and assemble the bowls just before serving to keep the ingredients fresh.

These Avocado and Veggie Sushi Bowls are not only delicious and colorful but also packed with nutrients and flavors reminiscent of your favorite sushi rolls. Enjoy the combination of creamy avocado, crisp vegetables, and savory sushi rice in each bite!

Spinach and Feta Stuffed Pastries

Ingredients:

- 1 package (about 10 sheets) phyllo dough, thawed if frozen
- 4 cups fresh spinach, chopped
- 1 tablespoon olive oil
- 1 small onion, finely chopped
- 2 cloves garlic, minced
- 1/2 cup crumbled feta cheese
- 1/4 cup grated Parmesan cheese
- Salt and pepper, to taste
- 1/4 teaspoon nutmeg (optional)
- 2 tablespoons melted butter or olive oil, for brushing

Instructions:

1. Prepare the filling:
    - Heat olive oil in a large skillet over medium heat. Add chopped onion and sauté until translucent, about 3-4 minutes.
    - Add minced garlic and chopped spinach to the skillet. Cook for another 2-3 minutes until spinach is wilted. Remove from heat and let cool slightly.
    - Stir in crumbled feta cheese, grated Parmesan cheese, salt, pepper, and nutmeg (if using). Mix well to combine.
2. Assemble the pastries:
    - Preheat your oven to 375°F (190°C). Line a baking sheet with parchment paper.
    - Place one sheet of phyllo dough on a clean work surface and brush lightly with melted butter or olive oil. Place another sheet on top and brush again with butter or oil (repeat with one more sheet if desired for thicker pastry).
    - Cut the layered phyllo dough into 4 equal squares or rectangles.
3. Fill and fold:
    - Place a spoonful of the spinach and feta mixture in the center of each phyllo square. Fold over one corner to the opposite corner to form a triangle or rectangle shape, depending on how you cut the dough.
    - Press the edges together to seal the filling inside the pastry. Repeat with remaining phyllo dough and filling.
4. Bake:
    - Place the stuffed pastries on the prepared baking sheet. Brush the tops with more melted butter or oil.
    - Bake in the preheated oven for 15-20 minutes, or until the pastries are golden brown and crispy.
5. Serve:
    - Remove from the oven and let cool slightly before serving.
    - Enjoy these Spinach and Feta Stuffed Pastries warm as a delicious appetizer or snack.

Tips:

- Phyllo Dough Handling: Work quickly with phyllo dough and keep unused sheets covered with a damp towel to prevent drying out.
- Variations: Add chopped sun-dried tomatoes, pine nuts, or herbs like dill or parsley to the filling for extra flavor.
- Make-Ahead: You can assemble the pastries ahead of time and refrigerate or freeze them before baking. Just bake from frozen, adding a few extra minutes to the baking time.

These Spinach and Feta Stuffed Pastries are crispy on the outside and filled with a savory spinach and cheese mixture inside, making them a delightful treat for any occasion. Enjoy making and serving these delicious pastries!

Veggie Frittata Muffins

Ingredients:

- 6 large eggs
- 1/4 cup milk (dairy or non-dairy)
- Salt and pepper, to taste
- 1 cup mixed vegetables, diced (e.g., bell peppers, spinach, tomatoes, mushrooms, onions)
- 1/2 cup grated cheese (cheddar, mozzarella, or your favorite)
- Optional add-ins: cooked diced ham, crumbled bacon, or cooked sausage
- Cooking spray or olive oil, for greasing the muffin tin

Instructions:

1. Preheat the oven and prepare muffin tin:
    - Preheat your oven to 350°F (175°C). Grease a 12-cup muffin tin with cooking spray or olive oil.
2. Prepare the egg mixture:
    - In a large bowl, whisk together eggs and milk until well combined. Season with salt and pepper to taste.
3. Prepare the filling:
    - Chop and prepare your choice of mixed vegetables and any optional add-ins.
4. Assemble the muffins:
    - Divide the mixed vegetables and cheese evenly among the muffin cups. If using optional add-ins like ham or bacon, distribute them as well.
5. Pour in the egg mixture:
    - Pour the egg mixture evenly into each muffin cup, filling almost to the top.
6. Bake:
    - Bake in the preheated oven for 20-25 minutes, or until the frittata muffins are puffed up, set in the center, and lightly golden on top.
7. Cool and serve:
    - Allow the frittata muffins to cool in the tin for a few minutes before carefully removing them with a spoon or knife. Serve warm or at room temperature.

Tips:

- Variations: Customize these muffins with your favorite vegetables and cheeses. Try adding herbs like parsley or basil for extra flavor.
- Storage: Store leftovers in an airtight container in the refrigerator for up to 3 days. Reheat in the microwave for a quick breakfast or snack.

These Veggie Frittata Muffins are portable, versatile, and packed with protein and nutrients from the eggs and vegetables. They make a perfect make-ahead breakfast or a healthy snack option on the go. Enjoy experimenting with different vegetable combinations to suit your taste!

Roasted Vegetable and Hummus Wraps

Ingredients:

- 1 large red bell pepper, sliced
- 1 medium zucchini, sliced
- 1 medium yellow squash, sliced
- 1 small red onion, sliced
- 2 tablespoons olive oil
- Salt and pepper, to taste
- 4 large whole wheat or spinach tortillas
- 1 cup hummus (store-bought or homemade)
- Handful of baby spinach or mixed greens
- Optional: crumbled feta cheese, sliced avocado, sun-dried tomatoes, sprouts

Instructions:

1. Preheat the oven:
    - Preheat your oven to 400°F (200°C).
2. Prepare the vegetables:
    - Place sliced red bell pepper, zucchini, yellow squash, and red onion on a baking sheet.
    - Drizzle with olive oil and season with salt and pepper. Toss to coat evenly.
3. Roast the vegetables:
    - Roast in the preheated oven for 20-25 minutes, or until vegetables are tender and lightly browned. Stir halfway through cooking for even roasting.
4. Assemble the wraps:
    - Warm the tortillas briefly in the microwave or oven to make them pliable.
    - Spread each tortilla with a generous layer of hummus.
5. Add roasted vegetables and greens:
    - Divide the roasted vegetables evenly among the tortillas, placing them in a line down the center of each tortilla.
    - Top with a handful of baby spinach or mixed greens.
6. Optional toppings:
    - Add crumbled feta cheese, sliced avocado, sun-dried tomatoes, or sprouts for extra flavor and texture.
7. Wrap it up:
    - Fold in the sides of each tortilla, then roll up tightly from the bottom to enclose the filling.
8. Serve:
    - Cut each wrap in half diagonally and serve immediately.

Tips:

- Variations: You can use any favorite vegetables for roasting such as eggplant, cherry tomatoes, or mushrooms.
- Protein Boost: Add grilled chicken strips, tofu, or chickpeas for extra protein.
- Make-Ahead: Prepare the roasted vegetables ahead of time and store them in the refrigerator. Assemble the wraps just before serving to keep them fresh.

These Roasted Vegetable and Hummus Wraps are not only delicious but also packed with healthy ingredients. They make a satisfying lunch or dinner option and are perfect for meal prepping or packing for lunch on the go. Enjoy the combination of roasted vegetables, creamy hummus, and fresh greens wrapped in a whole wheat tortilla!

www.ingramcontent.com/pod-product-compliance
Lightning Source LLC
LaVergne TN
LVHW081619060526
838201LV00054B/2317